One day
A very first dictionary

Ann James

For Mum

Melbourne
Oxford University Press
Oxford   Auckland   New York

One day . . .

Aa   # Bb

I woke up.

Cc   Dd

I got dressed.

Ee   Ff

I ate my breakfast.

Gg

Hh

I played outside.

Ii Jj

I ate my lunch.

Kk   Ll

I played inside.

Mm   Nn

I had a nap.

Oo   Pp

I went shopping.

Qq   Rr

I ran through the park.

Ss   Tt

I went to playgroup.

Uu   Vv

I ate my dinner.

Ww   Xx

I had a bath.

Yy	Zz

I read a story, and

I went to bed.